Topiary
for Kids

Louella Odié

SAGE
PRESS

Published in 2005

Text and Illustrations © Louella Odié
Design © Sage Press 2005

Set in Palatine italic 10 on 12 point leading.
Display in Palatino Light Italic 48 point.

Graphic Design
Chris Monk of Yellowduck Design Ltd

Text and Illustrations
Louella Odié

Series Editor and Publisher
Mrs Bobby Meyer

Printed in England

ISBN: 0-95 42297-9-7

SAGE PRESS
PO Box N° 1, Rye, East Sussex TN36 6HN.
e.mail: sagepress.bm@btinternet.com   www.treefinders.co.uk

| Toe | Pea | Prince Harry |

Introduction

'What on earth is topiary?', you might be saying if you have just been given this book as a present .

I expect if you **have** just been given this book it is because you are interested in gardening and growing things.
Topiary is the art of trimming plants into three-dimensional shapes. The shapes can be HUGE and old and formal, or they can be quirky and quite quick to make. It can be a way of expressing something of your own personality in a garden. It is a hobby that can be great fun and some people get completely carried away by their enthusiasm for it.
BUT (there is always a but isn't there?), the really frustrating thing about the traditional way of making topiary is that a good specimen can take quite a while to grow and that can be b-o-r-l-n-g.

So, to while away the time I have also included some craft projects in this little book, for rainy days and which produce instant results.

Five thousand years ago ancient farmers, training their grape vines for wine production realised that by pruning and clipping other plants in the same way they treated their vines, they could change the shape of its growth.

The first topiary was thought to be a stilt hedge (also known as pleaching – *see glossary*).
You can see how similar to grape growing it is.

During the Dark Ages the skill of topiary was continued in the monasteries of Italy. There they developed the idea of the maze. Instead of being a fun garden puzzle, their

Early topiary

mazes were only knee-high and a teaching aid. The young monks would have to develop their patience and demonstrate their devotion by enduring the frustrations of all the wrong turns and dead ends as they tried to get through the maze, even though they could easily step over the hedges. Giving up was considered shameful. These low hedge features eventually became knot gardens while mazes became taller.

Simple geometric shapes were added in the sixteenth century and topiary became more decorative. At Hampton Court, King Henry VIII was adding figurative topiary to his maze.

Hedges were clipped to form tunnels and archways and arranged to form 'walks' which were lawn passageways between private screening hedges. These were welcome places for privacy in large, crowded households and were perfect places to gossip and tell secrets.

Knot gardens had become as complicated as embroidery with all the spaces between the hedges filled with flowers and different textured foliage. This was the golden age of topiary. It became more symbolic and was used as a visual puzzle which viewers were able to solve. Around this time topiary chess pieces became popular. William of Orange became King of England in 1688 and he brought the Dutch style of topiary to England. This included a more light-hearted style and more animal shapes. Soon, such ideas spread to America.

Topiary became unfashionable in the early eighteenth century with the rise in popularity of a more naturalistic and freer style of garden and landscape. Of course, topiary was not completely abandoned and it had another rise in popularity with the Victorians. It is becoming very popular again today, perhaps because even in a small garden it lends a sense of formality and looks good all year round.

In ancient Rome topiary was a sign of status

Choosing suitable plants

Many plants will respond well to clipping and reward you by developing an interesting shape once clipped. But some are of course better than others.

Evergreen shrubs are most effective. They have small leaves and include box, yew, lonicera nitida, myrtle, and some types of conifer.

Next best would be evergreen plants that have bigger leaves. These are good, but are not suitable for making small shapes. The surface that you end up with will be more shaggy than smooth – this may not matter though if you want to make a yak instead of a sheep shape. Viburnum, holly, laurel and bay, for instance, also have flowers or berries. If you are clever and don't go mad with the shears it is possible to have a topiary shape AND flowers.

The third category of plants lose their leaves in winter. But their twigs and branches are attractive. I think that a large animal shape made from beech or hornbeam which keep some leaves in winter and turn a beautiful coppery-brown would be very effective.

Other plants which are not suitable for making complicated animal shapes can be clipped into very simple balls – very effective and quite satisfying to do. These include perennials such as santolina, lavender, the curry plant and rosemary .

What shape shall I cut?

I know if it were me, I would want to grab a pair of shears, rush outside and start hacking about on a big plant. Sadly I have never been allowed to do this and I would be most surprised if you will be either. Gardeners have to learn to be patient so consider this part of the challenge. Have a look outside in the places that you are allowed to garden and see if you are lucky enough to have a bit of lonicera nitida hedging. Lots of older houses have it: it is wonderful stuff and is also known as poor man's box. Perhaps the 'poor man' is not someone without money but someone responsible for keeping it in check — it grows so fast that it needs clipping almost every week. This makes it a good plant to practise on.

Now, if you **do** have some in the garden or if you have a plant in a pot that you have bought, take your time to consider what shape might be lurking in there. This thinking time is important regardless of which type of plant you are going to cut and it becomes VERY important if the plant is slow-growing and expensive like box or yew.

If your plant has never been
trimmed it might be quite
unkempt, with long
branches some of
which are quite long,
weak and bendy.

Take me to your leader!

Has your plant got a strong leader? This is a main stem that is stronger, straighter and hopefully more upright than the others. If it does, then you can make

some of these shapes: cones, spirals, standards.

If the plant does not have a strong leader, have a look and see if the growth is roughly the same 'strength' all over – ask yourself is the plant mound-shaped?

If it is, you could easily clip it into a ball shape which is not as dull as it might sound. Maybe you are a patient and clever sort of person, in which case you could cut it into a ball, allow it to thicken up for a bit and then carry on growing it into something different. Other shapes you can aim for are cones (perhaps supported on canes) and also simple blob shapes such as cats sitting down or rabbits. In both cases first form the body and later choose suitable shoots as they grow out, to train into ears.

If you notice that your plant grows faster on the top, say, and slower on the sides, or if it has a natural sort of parting, you probably have something that could be made into a bird, chicken or peacock.

Rule One

Rule Two

Rule Three

A Guide to Clipping

First rule of topiary: where you cut, more shoots will grow. This is important to remember because that is how you will get a shape to thicken up and spread out.

Second rule of topiary, where you want a straight line you may need to use a cane or stick to support it.

Third rule of topiary, where you want a curve you will need to tie the plant to a strong piece of wire.

Fourth rule of topiary, most complicated shapes require canes *and* wires (and several pairs of hands).

Fifth rule of topiary, mistakes will happen and things will usually grow back. ***Please note this does not apply to fingers. Read the safety rules on the inside front cover.***

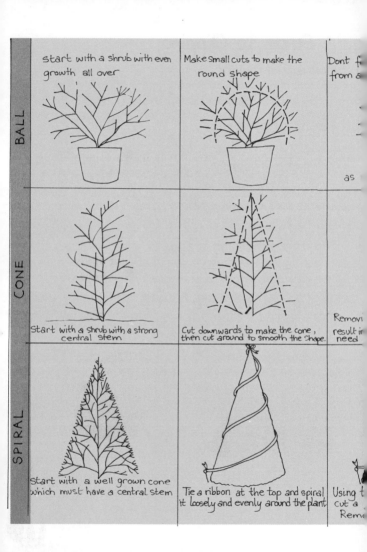

BALL

start with a shrub with even growth all over

Make small cuts to make the round shape

Dont f
from a

as

CONE

Start with a shrub with a strong central stem

Cut downwards to make the cone, then cut around to smooth the shape.

Removi
result ir
need

SPIRAL

Start with a well grown cone which must have a central stem

Tie a ribbon at the top and spiral it loosely and evenly around the plant

Using t
cut a
Reme

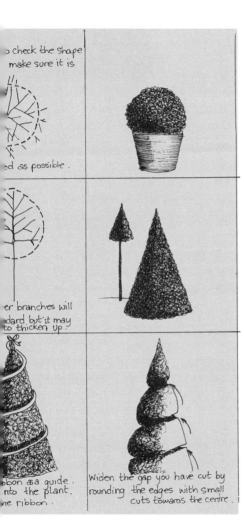

o check the shape
make sure it is

ed as possible.

er branches will
dard but it may
to thicken up.

bbon as a guide.
nto the plant.
ne ribbon.

Widen the gap you have cut by
rounding the edges with small
cuts towards the centre.

Ready ...
Steady ...
GO !

Now that you have studied your plant and know what it might be capable of you can start to trim. Follow the illustrations and be brave. Remember that most plants will recover and given enough time will return to much the same state that you found them in. This could even mean that with a fairly quick growing specimen it could have a couple of different identities.

Instant Sponge Trees

This is a good project fro practising the art of trimming. Even though we will be using scissors instead of shears it is great fun seeing the shape appearing. You could make a collection of 'plants' just for decoration or perhaps as an aid to planning your ideal garden–as you can imagine how things will look in three dimensions.

If you have a doll's house you could use these sponge trees for the front garden. Slices of sponge could also be fitted together to make a maze. All your discarded bits of sponge painted green can be used as 'countryside' around a train set.

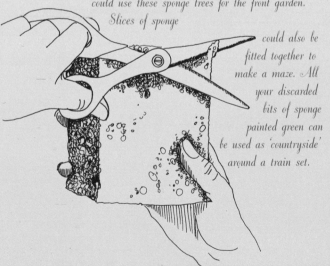

What You Need

- A large sponge — ideally one of those yellow car cleaning ones
- Pointy scissors
- Green poster paint and a brush
- A sharp stick or a pencil
- A suitable container to stand the stick in — a flower pot or a tin can
- Some gravel, sand or earth to hold the stick firmly

Method

- First and most importantly decide on what shape you are going to make. A cone shape is a good start.
- If you are worried about making a mistake you can draw the basic outline on one side of the sponge with a marker pen.
- Now take the scissors and begin to cut away at the places that you don't want. Make lots of small cuts rather than big ones.
- It is not a problem if you end up with a jagged surface or even if you cut into your line a little.
- Tip: Stop and look at what you are doing from time to time, it is very easy to get carried away and end up with something quite lop-sided.

If you do have a disaster just be glad it is only a sponge and not an expensive plant. You could try again, or cut your tree into a smaller shape. Creative people are allowed to change their minds so it doesn't really count as a mistake.

■ When you have reduced your sponge to a triangular shape, begin to make little cuts around the triangle to remove the hard angled edges. If you keep doing this, eventually you will end up with a rounded cone. It is hard to make the cone completely spherical because of the thickness of the sponge; two of the sides will be a little flatter. If an even shape is important to you, the two choices are: either make the shape very small so that the diameter of the cone will fit in, or stick two sponges together before you begin.

■ If there are too many cut marks and you think it doesn't look plant-like enough, you can also pull little bits off with your fingers which gives a different texture altogether.

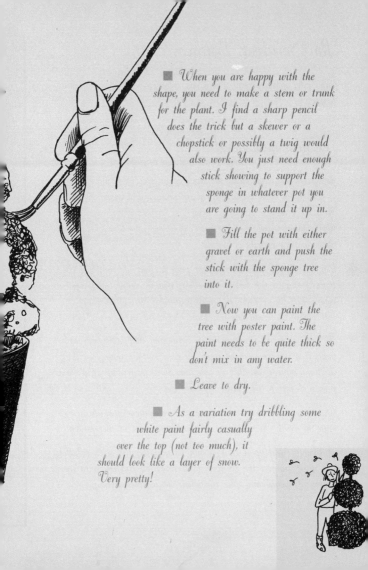

■ When you are happy with the shape, you need to make a stem or trunk for the plant. I find a sharp pencil does the trick but a skewer or a chopstick or possibly a twig would also work. You just need enough stick showing to support the sponge in whatever pot you are going to stand it up in.

■ Fill the pot with either gravel or earth and push the stick with the sponge tree into it.

■ Now you can paint the tree with poster paint. The paint needs to be quite thick so don't mix in any water.

■ Leave to dry.

■ As a variation try dribbling some white paint fairly casually over the top (not too much), it should look like a layer of snow. Very pretty!

Pan Scrubber Pictures

This is a quick project where you create a card with a garden theme.

What you need

- Green scouring pads. The cheap ones are better than the expensive ones, because they are thinner and easier to cut.
- PVA glue
- Coloured Card
- Colouring pencils or paints

Cut out shapes from the scourer pads to look like some of the topiary shapes you have seen. These can be simple ones, such as cones or balls, or more figurative animals. An interesting alternative is to cut out the same shape but in different sizes.

When you have a selection, try arranging them on your card to suggest a garden or landscape. Remember that shapes in the distance appear smaller, so you may have to arrange your biggest pieces closest to the bottom of the card.

When you are satisfied with your arrangement glue the pieces onto the card. Then sketch in or paint the rest of the garden.

I like to build up a bit of depth by layering the pads, but then you must support the scourers underneath by padding with more layers of sponge and glue the whole lot together firmly.

draw and Colour
the rest of the
garden.

Cut off the
part that
overlaps
so that
you
can glue
it flat

make this
part curved
so that it looks
more realistic

mple shapes
en assemble
to make up
e 3-dimensional
e.

An old wire frame from a lampshade may not look like much on its own, but if it is strong enough it could perhaps support a basket of flowers

 What could you make with a pair of old bicycle wheels?

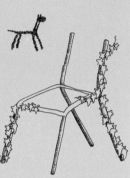

Can you imagine how to transform an old metal chair frame into an animal shape? You might need wire for the tail and the head

An old supermarket basket covered in ivy would look lovely with pots of winter-flowering pansies or polyanthus

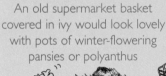

Frames using 'found objects'

The are many wire topiary frames for sale and you may be lucky and be given one. They can look like a chicken wire cage in the shape of an animal which you place over your small plant, or they may be a simple wire outline. The cage ones are easier to use because right from the start you can imagine how your plant will look when it has grown to fill up the space inside.

But bought frames are not really necessary and it can be great fun to find or make your own. I think the big disadvantage of the bought frames is that you can't change your mind about the shape you are planning to grow. If you have been given a chicken shape that is what you will have to grow – you can't let the tail end grow and turn it into a peacock or extend the neck and make a pheasant or a goose.

The illustrations (opposite page) show what you might be able to find to make into a shape.

The most important thing to remember with found frames is that they might have sharp edges, **so do beware**. Also think about how much light the plant will have while it is adapting to the frame. If it is too dark, beneath a table for example, it will not grow well.

Ivy

In a book about topiary you might expect that it would be all about cutting shrubs but in fact you can train climbers into shapes even more easily than you can bushy plants. And the best climber for this is IVY !

Ivy is a fantastic plant to grow: it's cheap to buy when it is small, and it is easy to take a cutting so you may not have to buy any at all. It grows quite fast and it comes with lots of different leaf shapes, markings and colours. Lastly it loves being trained over things.

Just as with the other plants you get a more recognisable shape and a smoother texture if you use smaller leaf varieties, the same is true of ivy. But the choice is up to you. Even the common dark green garden ivy is suitable for training – so have a go with whatever you can find!

Making an Ivy heart

This makes a fantastic and easy present for Valentine's Day. Any ivy is suitable but the smaller the leaves the better you can see the shape.

What you need

- A wire coat hanger
- Pliers
- Garden twine
- A 9 cm flowerpot planted with trailing ivy

To start with you must turn your wire coat hanger into a topiary frame. It is not difficult to see how this might be done but it can take a bit of wrestling to do so. That is why you might need the pliers. You might also need a strong grown-up, depending on your age, which of course I cannot see from here.

■ Bend the hook of the hanger into as straight a line as you can. This will support the heart shape when it is pushed into the flowerpot.

■ Next you turn the shoulders of the hanger into as round a shape as you can — try putting your foot on it and pulling.

■ When you have a two-dimensional lollipop shape you can push it in at the top to make the dip in the middle of the heart. Keep fiddling with it until you get a shape you like.

■ When you are satisfied, push the straightened wire hook into the centre of the ivy planted in the flowerpot. Ideally the bottom of the heart will begin just above the top of the ivy. If you want to make a shape that is more like a standard, i.e. it has a stem; you will need to support this with a cane.

■ Now carefully sort out your ivy trails and tie them to the heart individually with little bits of twine. Take some to the left and some to the right. Do not wind them round and round the wire. The tying-in is important, because otherwise the ivy will eventually strangle itself.

■ Trim back any trails that are too long and any which you think are pointing in the wrong direction. That's it!

■ Now you just need to keep your plant fed and watered. Keep trimming back any stems that start going off in the wrong direction and tying-in the ones you want to keep. Gradually the ivy will thicken up and the shape will become more and more solid.

Mazes

Mazes are a fascinating subject and could easily fill a book of their own. Some people spend their whole life admiring the mathematical complexities which inventing a maze can present. They can of course be made out of all sorts of things and some of the earliest ones by the ancient Egyptians were actually three-dimensional puzzles constructed though buildings with hidden passages and tunnels. Hedge mazes came a bit later. We tend to think of them as a big garden puzzle – which of course they are when you are lost in them. But they were also planted in mediaeval times to represent a spiritual journey through life. The meaning behind all the twists, turns and dead ends was that by choosing the correct path you would reach your goal of going to heaven.

You don't need a ten foot high hedge maze to recreate this spiritual journey of course. Some mazes were built without walls at all – these could be made from turf and were often a series of concentric circles, one within the other, just made from different heights of cut grass. You follow the path of the cut grass as you make your way to the centre.

Mustard and cress maze

What you need

- A waterproof baking tray would do or a grow-bag tray is even better.
- Mustard and cress seeds.
- Some hideous swirly pattern material or some white sketchbook paper
- Some newspapers (not today's).

- Lay several sheets of newspaper in the tray — neatly so that the base is covered and it is quite flat.
- If you are using the swirly fabric cut it to fit in the tray.
- If you are using plain white paper scribble all over it with a pencil or biro — not felt pen, and then cut it to fit inside the tray.
- Now water the whole thing so that it is thoughly damp, drain off any puddles — it might be best to do this part of the project outside.

- Make sure your hands are dry and tip your mustard and cress seeds into a bowl.
- Get comfortable because the next bit takes a bit of time.
- Taking small pinches of seeds try and

I'm worried a big egg sandwich is going to get us

LOST IN THE MUSTARD AND CRESS MAZE

drop them, a few at a time, along the lines of the swirly pattern or along the lines of your scribble. Larger areas can be filled in with more seeds but don't overdo it as they will swell up and spread out when they are growing.

■ You don't need to follow every line especially if the pattern is small. It is only meant to act as a guide. In fact it is a good idea to leave a path that is at least an inch wide to allow for the growth of the seeds. Make up the pattern of the maze as you go along and don't worry about lines ending.

■ Keep your mini-maze damp and watch as the seeds begin to grow.

■ When it has got big enough you can trim your 'hedges'.

This works with grass seed too and if your tray is big enough you can add gravel or sand or soil to the paths between the seeds and make it as realistic as you like.

I use to love making mazes like this when I was little. My sister and I would catch creepy-crawlies and put them in the maze and then make up stories pretending that they were lost. We built them little mud houses too. Of course we always let them go in the end...

Knot gardens

Mazes take up a lot of space but it *is* possible to squeeze a knot garden into a small area.

In a knot garden the idea is to keep the planting very low so that the impact of the design can be see from above. The pattern can be very complicated and intricate with the plants appearing to weave over and under each other. Just as attractive is a simple design. Perhaps using the initials of your name.

Traditionally box was used for knot gardens but any plant of low height is suitable and it could be fun to think of some alternative schemes. Parsley would be good, also different colours of thyme could be used for different parts of a pattern. Even ivy is effective; pin it down to the ground using wire loops to form

'I'm not going if it's violent'

your design and then keep trimming it back when it starts to grow. Quite quickly you will see that it starts to form a little rope-like hedge and with all the different colours of variegation available it could be quite beautiful.

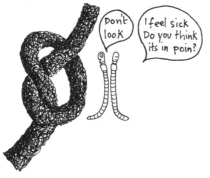

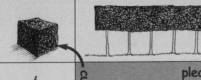

 cube

cone

wedding stand

clouds

freestyle

pleached or stilt hedge

Glossary

Deciduous a plant that has foliage only during the growing season and becomes dormant over winter

Evergreen a plant that does not lose its leaves during the winter

Figurative topiary that is trying to look like something other than a plant, for example a chicken

Leader the central stem of a plant or tree

Patience the quality of being able to put up with delay, in this case the very slow growth of some plants

Parterre an arrangement of flower beds being laid out in a pattern and possibly with low hedges enclosing what is grown in the bed

 freestyle

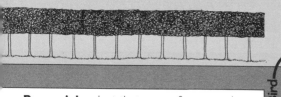

Perennial a plant that grows for more than one season, and usually for several years

Pleached a method of training trees or hedges where the branches are tied to posts and wires sideways and usually at head-height, linking the row of plants. This gives the effect of trees in line holding hands

Topiary the clipping of plants into a shape that it would not have grown into naturally

About the author and illustrator

Louella, artist and illustrator, is also a keen gardener and caught the topiary bug from Judy Older and is now equally obsessive. If you have a space in your garden The Two Blonde Clippers (Judy and Louella) will fill it – preferably with something amusing.

To contact: Louella Tel: 07968-029542
louellaodiedesign@yahoo.com

Bird

ball

spiral

poodle

hedge with arch and window

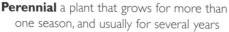

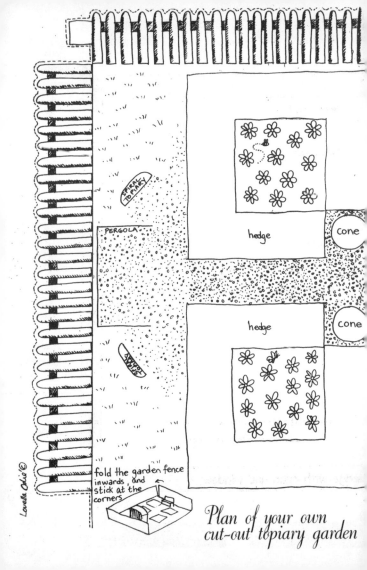

SPIRAL TOPIARY

PERGOLA

hedge

cone

hedge

cone

fold the garden fence inwards, and stick at the corners

Lovella Okiè ©

Plan of your own cut-out topiary garden

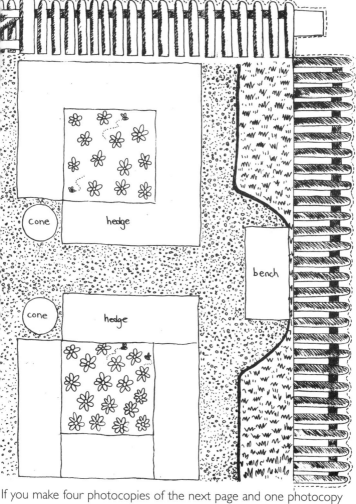

If you make four photocopies of the next page and one photocopy of this garden plan,you can assemble your own parterre. I recommend you photcopy onto thickish paper and enlarge the image by 100%.Stick the pieces together with glue or tape.

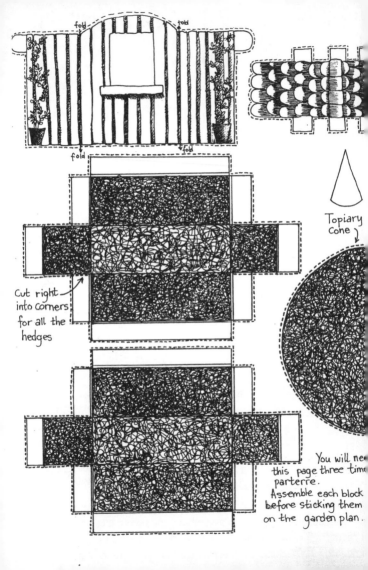

fold   fold

fold   fold

Cut right
into corners
for all the
hedges

Topiary
Cone

You will nee
this page three time
parterre.
Assemble each block
before sticking them
on the garden plan.

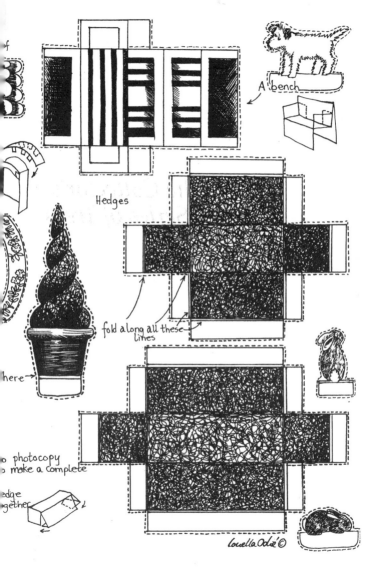

A bench

Hedges

fold along all these lines

here→

photocopy
make a complete

edge
ogether

Louella Odie©

The Collector's Series of Trees

Are you collecting…?

"… and a very charming book it is…"
Roy Lancaster,
on MONKEY PUZZLE